COOKIES
FOR ALL OCCASIONS

Publications International, Ltd.

Favorite Brand Name Recipes at www.fbnr.com

Some of the products listed in this publication may be in limited distribution.

Recipe Development: Recipes on pages 26, 28, 30, 38, 56, 58, 72, 82, 92, 94, 96, 98, 100, 102, 104 and 110 by Cynthia M. Colby.

Photography on pages 27, 29, 31, 39, 47, 57, 59, 73, 83, 93, 95, 97, 99, 101, 103, 105 and 111 by Proffitt Photography Ltd., Chicago.
Photographer: Laurie Proffitt
Photographer's Assistant: Sarah Gilbert
Prop Stylist: Paula Walters
Food Stylist: Teri Rys-Maki
Assistant Food Stylist: Lezli Bitterman

Pictured on the front cover *(clockwise from top left):* Fireside Cookie *(page 74),* Lady Bugs *(page 48),* Festive Easter Cookies *(page 34)* and Cookie Pizza *(page 120).*

Pictured on the back cover *(clockwise from top left):* High-Flying Flags *(page 46),* Mini Wedding Cakes *(page 100),* Myrtle the Turtle *(page 110)* and Congrats Grad! *(page 98).*

ISBN: 0-7853-6154-5

Library of Congress Control Number: 2001096916

Manufactured in China.

8 7 6 5 4 3 2 1

Microwave Cooking: Microwave ovens vary in wattage. Use the cooking times as guidelines and check for doneness before adding more time.

Contents

Fun with Cookies

basic cookie tips

- Read the entire recipe before beginning to make sure you have all the necessary ingredients, baking utensils and supplies.

- For the best results, use the ingredients called for in the recipe. Butter, margarine and shortening are not always interchangeable.

- Follow the recipe directions and baking times exactly. Check for doneness using the test given in the recipe. Most cookies bake quickly, so check them at the minimum baking time, then watch carefully to make sure they don't burn.

- Measure all the ingredients accurately and assemble them in the order they are called for in the recipe.

- For easier handling, chill cookie dough for cutouts before rolling. Remove only enough dough from the refrigerator to work with at one time. Save any trimmings and reroll them all at once to prevent the dough from becoming tough.

- Adjust the oven racks and preheat the oven. Check the oven temperature for accuracy with an oven thermometer.

- Cookies that are uniform in size and shape will finish baking at the same time.

- Space unbaked cookies about 2 inches apart on the cookie sheets to allow for spreading, unless the recipe directs otherwise.

- Many cookies should be removed from the cookie sheets immediately after baking and placed in a single layer on wire racks to cool. Fragile cookies may need to cool slightly on the cookie sheet before being removed to wire racks to cool completely.

- Unbaked dough can be refrigerated for up to two weeks or frozen for up to six weeks. Rolls of dough should be wrapped tightly in plastic wrap; other doughs should be stored in airtight containers. Label the dough with baking information for convenience.

making patterns for cutouts

When a pattern for a cutout cookie is to be used only once, make the pattern out of waxed paper. Using the photo or diagram as a guide, draw the pattern pieces on waxed paper. Cut the pieces out and place them on the rolled-out cookie dough. Carefully cut around the pattern pieces with a sharp knife. Remove the pattern pieces from the dough and discard. Continue as directed in the recipe.

For patterns that are used more than once, make the pattern more durable by using clean, lightweight cardboard or poster board. Using the photo or diagram as a guide, draw the pattern pieces on the cardboard. Cut the pieces out and lightly spray one side with nonstick cooking spray. Place the pattern pieces, sprayed side down, on the rolled-out dough; cut around them with a sharp knife. Reuse the pattern pieces to make as many cutouts as needed.

melting chocolate

Make sure the utensils you use for melting chocolate are completely dry. Moisture makes chocolate become stiff and grainy. If this happens, add ½ teaspoon shortening (not butter) for each ounce of chocolate and stir until smooth. Chocolate scorches easily and cannot be used once it is scorched. Follow one of these three methods for successful melting.

Double Boiler: This is the safest method because it prevents scorching. Place the chocolate in the top of a double boiler or in a bowl over hot, not boiling, water; stir until smooth. (Make sure the water remains just below a simmer and is one inch below the top pan.) Be careful that no steam or water gets into the chocolate.

Direct Heat: Place the chocolate in a heavy saucepan and melt it over very low heat, stirring constantly. Remove the chocolate from the heat as soon as it is melted. Be sure to watch the chocolate carefully since it is easily scorched with this method.

Microwave Oven: Place 4 to 6 unwrapped 1-ounce squares of chocolate or 1 cup of chocolate chips in a small microwavable bowl. Microwave at HIGH (100% power) for 1 to 1½ minutes. Stir after 1 minute and at 30-second intervals after the first minute. Repeat the procedure as necessary to melt the chocolate. Be sure to stir the microwaved chocolate because it can retain its original shape even when melted.

piping techniques

For each of the following piping techniques, you'll need a pastry bag (also called a decorating bag) fitted with the appropriate decorating tip and filled with frosting. If you will be using different tips when decorating, a coupler will make changing tips much easier.

A coupler is used to attach tips to the pastry bag and allows you to change tips without removing the frosting from the bag. To use, unscrew the ring; insert the cone-shaped piece into the narrow end of an empty pastry bag until the narrow end extends slightly beyond the end of the bag (snip off the end of the pastry bag if necessary). Place the coupler ring over the decorating tip. Screw the ring on to hold the tip in place. To change tips, unscrew the ring, remove the tip, replace with the new tip and screw the ring back in place.

To fill a pastry bag, insert the decorating tip or attach the tip with a coupler. Fold the top of the bag down and place the frosting in the bag. In general, fill the bag half to two-thirds full, then unfold the top of the bag. Twist the top of the bag tightly against the frosting.

Place the twisted end of the bag in the palm of your writing hand with your fingers positioned near the bag opening. Place your other hand under the bag to guide the tip as shown.

When piping, hold the bag so the tip is at the angle indicated for the technique. Then, gently squeeze the bag from the top, using even pressure while guiding the tip with your other hand. Squeeze mainly with the palm of your hand rather than your fingers. Be careful not to loosen your grip on the twisted end or the frosting will begin to push up and out of the top of the bag.

Line (use writing or small open star tip): Hold bag so tip is at a 45° angle to the right. While gently squeezing bag, guide tip opening just above cookie in a curved, zigzag, squiggly or straight line. To end line, stop squeezing, then lift tip.

Dot (use round tip): Hold bag so tip is at a 90° angle. Position opening just above the cookie and gently squeeze. Lift slightly while still squeezing. When dot is desired size, stop squeezing, then lift tip. To pipe a dot border, position tip almost touching first dot and pipe another dot. Repeat to complete border.

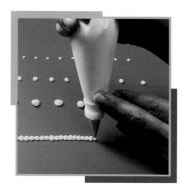

Writing (use writing tip): Hold bag so tip is at a 45° angle to the right for horizontal lines and toward you for vertical lines. While gently squeezing bag, guide tip opening just above cookie to form print or script letters. Stop squeezing, then lift tip at the end of each letter for print letters and at the end of each word for script writing.

Star (use open or closed star tip): Hold bag so tip is at a 90° angle. Position opening just above the cookie and gently squeeze. Lift slightly while still squeezing. When star is desired size, stop squeezing, then lift tip. To pipe a star border, position tip almost touching first star and pipe another star. Repeat to complete border.

Shell (use round tip, or open or closed star tip): Hold bag so tip is at a 45° angle to the right just above the cookie. Squeeze until a small mound is formed for base of shell, lifting slightly. Continue squeezing with lighter pressure while pulling tip away from base to the right until tail is desired length. Stop squeezing, then lift tip. To pipe a shell border, position tip almost touching tail of first shell and pipe another shell. Repeat to complete border.

*A*nyday treats

cheery chocolate animal cookies

1⅔ cups (10-ounce package) **REESE'S® Peanut Butter Chips**

1 cup **HERSHEY'S Semi-Sweet Chocolate Chips**

2 tablespoons shortening (do not use butter, margarine, spread or oil)

1 package (20 ounces) chocolate sandwich cookies

1 package (11 ounces) animal crackers

1 Line trays or cookie sheets with wax paper. Combine peanut butter chips, chocolate chips and shortening in 2-quart glass measuring cup with handle. Microwave on HIGH (100% power) 1½ to 2 minutes or until chips are melted and mixture is smooth when stirred. Using fork, dip each cookie into melted chip mixture; gently tap fork on side of cup to remove excess chocolate.

2 Place coated cookies on prepared trays; top each cookie with an animal cracker. Chill until chocolate is set, about 30 minutes. Store in airtight container in a cool, dry place.

makes about 4 dozen cookies

cheery chocolate animal cookies

lollipop sugar cookies

1¼ cups granulated sugar

1 cup Butter Flavor CRISCO®
    all-vegetable shortening or
    1 Butter Flavor CRISCO®
    Stick

2 eggs

¼ cup light corn syrup or regular
    pancake syrup

1 tablespoon vanilla

3 cups all-purpose flour

¾ teaspoon baking powder

½ teaspoon baking soda

½ teaspoon salt

36 flat ice cream sticks

Any of the following: miniature
    baking chips, raisins, red hots,
    nonpareils, colored sugar or
    nuts

1 Combine sugar and shortening in large bowl. Beat at medium speed of electric mixer until well blended. Add eggs, syrup and vanilla; beat until well blended and fluffy.

2 Combine flour, baking powder, baking soda and salt. Add gradually to creamed mixture at low speed until well blended. Wrap dough in plastic wrap. Refrigerate at least 1 hour.

3 Heat oven to 375°F. Place foil on countertop for cooling cookies. Shape dough into 1½-inch balls. Push ice cream stick into center of each ball. Place balls 3 inches apart on ungreased baking sheet. Flatten balls to ½-inch thickness with bottom of greased and floured glass. Decorate as desired; press decorations gently into dough.*

4 Bake at 375°F for 8 to 10 minutes. *Do not overbake.* Cool on baking sheet 2 minutes. Remove cookies to foil to cool completely.

Cookies can also be painted before baking. Mix 1 egg yolk and ¼ teaspoon water. Divide into 3 small cups. Add 2 to 3 drops food color to each. Stir. Use clean water color brushes to paint designs on cookies.

makes about 3 dozen
cookies

lollipop sugar cookies

cookie tools

1 package (18 ounces) refrigerated chocolate cookie dough*

All-purpose flour (optional)

White Decorator Frosting (recipe follows)

Assorted food colors (optional)

Colored sprinkles

*If refrigerated chocolate cookie dough is unavailable, add 1/4 cup unsweetened cocoa powder to refrigerated sugar cookie dough. Beat in large bowl at high speed of electric mixer until well blended.

1 Preheat oven to 350°F. Remove dough from wrapper. Cut dough in half. Wrap one dough half in plastic wrap; refrigerate.

2 Roll remaining dough on lightly floured surface to 1/8-inch thickness. Sprinkle with flour to minimize sticking, if necessary. Cut out tools using 4½- to 5-inch cookie cutters.* Place cookies 2 inches apart on ungreased cookie sheets. Repeat with remaining dough and scraps.

3 Bake 8 to 10 minutes or until firm, but not browned. Cool on cookie sheets 2 minutes. Remove to wire rack; cool completely.

4 Prepare White Decorator Frosting; tint with food colors, if desired. Spread frosting evenly over top of each cookie. Decorate as desired.

*If you do not have cookie cutters, create a pattern following the directions on page 5.

WHITE DECORATOR FROSTING: **Combine** 1 pound powdered sugar, ½ cup vegetable shortening, 1 tablespoon corn syrup and 6 tablespoons milk in bowl. Beat 2 minutes or until fluffy, adding additional milk if necessary.

makes 2 dozen cookies

cookie tools

our house

1 package (18 ounces) refrigerated cookie dough, any flavor

All-purpose flour (optional)

Blue, green, white and purple icings, granulated sugar, yellow-colored sugar, green gumdrops, red licorice, small decors and hard candies

SUPPLIES

Pastry bags and assorted decorating tips

1 Preheat oven to 350°F. Line large cookie sheet with parchment paper. Remove dough from wrapper. Roll small piece of dough into 1½-inch square; reserve.

2 Press remaining dough into 12×9-inch rectangle on prepared cookie sheet. Sprinkle with flour to minimize sticking, if necessary. Place reserved dough at top of rectangle to make chimney. Press to seal.

3 Bake 10 to 12 minutes or until edges are lightly browned. Cool on baking sheet 5 minutes. Slide house and parchment paper onto wire rack; cool completely.

4 Decorate as shown in photo. Use flat decorating tip for clapboards and shingles, yellow colored sugar for windows, star decorating tip for columns and steps, and gumdrops for bushes.

TIP: This is a perfect rainy-day project. Keep your kids entertained by decorating this cookie house as directed or let their minds go wild and decorate it however they like.

makes 1 large cookie

our house

sugar cookies

1 cup granulated sugar

1 cup butter, softened

2 eggs

½ teaspoon lemon extract

½ teaspoon vanilla

3 cups all-purpose flour

1 teaspoon baking powder

¼ teaspoon salt

EGG YOLK PAINT

2 egg yolks

2 teaspoons water

DECORATIONS

Royal Icing (page 34)

Decorator Frosting (recipe follows)

SUPPLIES

Liquid or paste food colors

Small, clean craft paintbrushes and clean kitchen sponges

Pastry bags and small writing tips

1 Beat sugar and butter in bowl until light. Beat in eggs and extracts. Beat in 1 cup flour, baking powder and salt. Beat in remaining 2 cups flour until soft dough forms. Divide dough into 3 discs; wrap in plastic wrap. Chill 2 hours or until firm.

2 Preheat oven to 375°F. Working with 1 disc at a time, unwrap dough and place on floured surface. Roll dough with rolling pin to ⅛-inch thickness. Cut out with lightly floured 3- to 4-inch cookie cutters. Place cutouts 1 inch apart on ungreased cookie sheets. Gently press dough trimmings together; reroll and cut out more cookies. (If dough is sticky, pat into disc; wrap in plastic wrap and refrigerate until firm before rerolling.)

3 To paint cookies before baking, prepare Egg Yolk Paint by combining egg yolks and water in small bowl with fork until blended. Divide paint among several bowls; tint with food colors, if desired. Paint yolk paint onto unbaked cookies with small, clean craft paintbrushes.

4 Bake 7 to 9 minutes or until cookies are set. Remove cookies to wire rack; cool completely.

makes 3 dozen cookies

sugar cookies

5 To sponge paint cooled cookies, prepare Royal Icing. Divide among several bowls; tint with food colors. For best results, use 2 to 3 shades of same color. (If icing is too thick, stir in water, 1 drop at a time until of desired consistency.) Spread thin icing layer on cookies. Let stand 30 minutes or until set. Cut clean sponge into 1-inch squares. Dip sponge into tinted icing, scraping off excess. Press sponge on base icing several times until desired effect is achieved. Let stand 15 minutes or until set.

6 To pipe additional decorations on cookies, prepare Decorator Frosting. Tint frosting as desired. Place each color frosting in pastry bag fitted with small writing tip or resealable plastic bags with one small corner cut off. Decorate as desired. Let cookies stand until piping is set.

DECORATOR FROSTING

¾ cup butter, softened

4½ cups powdered sugar, sifted

3 tablespoons water

1 teaspoon vanilla

¼ teaspoon lemon extract

Beat butter in medium bowl until smooth. Add 2 cups sugar. Beat until fluffy. Add water and extracts. Beat until blended, scraping down side of bowl once. Beat in remaining 2½ cups sugar until mixture is creamy. *Makes 2 cups*

cookie canvases

1 package (20 ounces) refrigerated cookie dough, any flavor

Cookie Glaze (recipe follows)

Assorted liquid food colors

SUPPLIES

1 (3½-inch) square cardboard template

1 (2½×4½-inch) rectangular cardboard template

Small, clean craft paintbrushes

1. Preheat oven to 350°F. Grease cookie sheets. Remove dough from wrapper. Cut dough in half. Wrap one dough half in plastic wrap; refrigerate.

2. Roll remaining dough on floured surface to ¼-inch thickness. Cut out cookie shapes using cardboard templates as guides. Place cookies 2 inches apart on prepared cookie sheets. Repeat steps with remaining dough.

3. Bake 8 to 10 minutes or until edges are browned. Remove from oven and straighten cookie edges. Cool on cookie sheets. Prepare Cookie Glaze.

4. Place cookies on wire racks set over waxed paper. Spread Cookie Glaze on cookies. Let stand at room temperature 40 minutes or until glaze is set. Place food colors in small bowls. Using clean craft paintbrushes, decorate cookies as desired with food colors by "painting" designs.

COOKIE GLAZE: Combine 4 cups powdered sugar and 4 tablespoons milk in bowl. Stir; add 1 to 2 tablespoons more milk as needed to make a medium-thick, pourable glaze.

makes 8 to 10 cookies

cookie canvases

musical instruments

1 package (18 ounces)
   refrigerated sugar cookie
   dough

All-purpose flour (optional)

Assorted colored frostings,
   colored gels, colored sugars,
   candies and small decors

1   Preheat oven to 350°F. Grease cookie sheets. Remove dough from wrapper. Cut dough in half. Wrap one dough half in plastic wrap; refrigerate.

2   Roll reserved dough on lightly floured surface to ¼-inch thickness. Sprinkle with flour to minimize sticking, if necessary. Cut out cookies using 3½-inch musical notes and instrument cookie cutters.* Place cutouts 2 inches apart on prepared cookie sheets. Repeat with remaining dough.

3   Bake 10 to 12 minutes or until edges are lightly browned. Remove from oven. Cool on cookie sheets 2 minutes. Remove to wire racks; cool completely.

4   Decorate with colored frostings, colored gels, colored sugars, candies and assorted decors as shown in photo or as desired.

*If you do not have cookie cutters, create a pattern following the directions on page 5.

makes 2 dozen cookies

Springtime pleasers

butterfly cookies

2¼ cups all-purpose flour

¼ teaspoon salt

1 cup sugar

¾ cup butter, softened

1 egg

1 teaspoon vanilla

1 teaspoon almond extract

White frosting, assorted food colors, colored sugars, small decors, gummy fruit and hard candies

1 Combine flour and salt in medium bowl; set aside. Beat sugar and butter in large bowl at medium speed of electric mixer until fluffy. Beat in egg, vanilla and almond extract. Gradually add flour mixture. Beat at low speed until well blended. Divide dough in half. Wrap each half in plastic wrap; refrigerate 30 minutes or until firm.

2 Preheat oven to 350°F. Grease cookie sheets. Roll half of dough on lightly floured surface to ¼-inch thickness. Cut out cookies using butterfly cookie cutters. Repeat with remaining dough.

3 Bake 12 to 15 minutes or until edges are lightly browned. Remove cookies to wire racks; cool completely.

4 Tint portions of white frosting with assorted food colors. Spread desired colors of frosting over cookies. Decorate with sugars, decors and candies as desired.

makes 20 to 22 cookies

butterfly cookies

shamrock ice cream sandwiches

Butter Cookie Dough (page 87)

Green food color

1 pint ice cream or frozen yogurt, any flavor

1 Prepare Butter Cookie Dough as directed, but do not wrap and chill dough. Tint dough with food color. Wrap in plastic wrap; refrigerate until firm, about 4 hours or overnight.

2 Preheat oven to 350°F. Roll dough on lightly floured surface to $1/4$-inch thickness. Cut out cookies using $3^{1}/_2$- to 5-inch shamrock-shaped cookie cutter. Place on ungreased cookie sheets.

3 Bake 8 to 10 minutes or until cookies are lightly browned around edges. Remove cookies to wire racks; cool completely.

4 Remove ice cream from freezer; let stand at room temperature to soften slightly, about 10 minutes. Spread 4 to 5 tablespoons ice cream onto flat sides of half the cookies. Place remaining cookies, flat sides down, on ice cream; press cookies together lightly.

5 Wrap each sandwich in foil; freeze until firm, about 2 hours or overnight. (Filled cookies store well up to 1 week in freezer.)

makes about
8 sandwich cookies

shamrock ice cream
sandwiches

pretty posies

I package (20 ounces)
    refrigerated sugar cookie
    dough

Orange and purple food colors

I tablespoon sprinkles

All-purpose flour (optional)

1 Remove dough from wrapper. Reserve $\frac{1}{6}$ of dough. Add orange food color and sprinkles to reserved dough until well blended; shape into $7\frac{1}{2}$-inch log. Wrap with plastic wrap and chill 30 minutes or until firm. Add purple food color to remaining dough until well blended. (If dough is too sticky, add flour as needed.) Wrap with plastic wrap and chill 30 minutes or until firm.

2 Roll out purple dough to $6\times7\frac{1}{2}$-inch rectangle on sheet of waxed paper. Place orange log in center of rectangle. Bring waxed paper and edges of purple dough up and over top of orange log; press gently. Overlap purple dough edges slightly; press gently. Wrap waxed paper around dough and twist ends to secure. Freeze log 20 minutes.

3 Preheat oven to 350°F. Grease cookie sheets. Remove waxed paper from dough log. Cut log with sharp knife into $\frac{1}{4}$-inch slices. Place 2 inches apart on prepared cookie sheets. Using 2- to $2\frac{1}{2}$-inch flower-shaped cookie cutter, cut slices into flowers; remove and discard dough scraps.

4 Bake 15 to 17 minutes or until edges are lightly browned. Remove cookies to wire racks; cool.

makes 1½ dozen cookies

pretty posies

springtime nests

1 cup butterscotch chips

½ cup light corn syrup

½ cup creamy peanut butter

⅓ cup sugar

2 cups corn flakes, slightly crushed

2½ cups chow mein noodles

Jelly beans or malted milk egg candies

1 Combine butterscotch chips, corn syrup, peanut butter and sugar in large microwavable bowl. Microwave at HIGH (100% power) 1 to 1½ minutes or until melted and smooth, stirring at 30-second intervals.

2 Stir in corn flakes and chow mein noodles until evenly coated. Quickly shape scant ¼ cupfuls mixture into balls; make indentation in centers to make nests. Place nests on waxed paper to set. Place 3 jelly beans in each nest.

makes 1½ dozen cookies

springtime nests

fluffy cottontails

½ cup unsalted butter, softened

½ cup shortening

¾ cup sugar

1 teaspoon vanilla

2 cups all-purpose flour

⅔ cup malted milk powder

¼ teaspoon salt

Malted milk balls

Miniature marshmallows

Assorted colored icings

1 Beat butter, shortening, sugar and vanilla in large bowl. Add flour, malted milk powder and salt until well blended.

2 Preheat oven to 350°F. Lightly grease cookie sheets. For bunny body, shape heaping teaspoonfuls of dough around malted milk balls. For bunny head, shape scant teaspoonfuls of dough into balls. Press body and head together on prepared cookie sheet. Shape ½ teaspoon dough into 2 ears; press gently into head.

3 Bake 8 minutes or until lightly browned. Let cookies cool 1 minute on cookie sheets. Remove to wire racks to cool completely.

4 Cut marshmallows in half. Decorate cookies using colored icings as desired. Immediately place marshmallow halves on cookies to resemble bunny tails. Let cookies stand until icing is set.

makes 2½ dozen cookies

fluffy cottontails

edible easter baskets

1 package (about 18 ounces)
    refrigerated sugar cookie
    dough

1 cup "M&M's"® Milk Chocolate
    Mini Baking Bits, divided

1 teaspoon water

1 to 2 drops green food coloring

¾ cup sweetened shredded
    coconut

¾ cup any flavor frosting

    Red licorice whips, cut into
    3-inch lengths

Lightly grease 36 (1¾-inch) mini muffin cups. Cut dough into 36 equal pieces; roll into balls. Place 1 ball in each muffin cup. Press dough onto bottom and up side of each muffin cup; chill 15 minutes. Press ⅓ cup "M&M's"® Milk Chocolate Mini Baking Bits into bottoms and sides of dough cups. Preheat oven to 350°F. Bake cookies 8 to 9 minutes. Cookies will be puffy. Remove from oven; gently press down center of each cookie. Return to oven 1 minute. Cool cookies in muffin cups 5 minutes. Remove to wire racks; cool completely. In medium bowl combine water and food coloring. Add coconut; stir until evenly tinted. In each cookie cup, layer 1 teaspoon frosting, 1 teaspoon tinted coconut and 1 teaspoon "M&M's"® Milk Chocolate Mini Baking Bits. Push both licorice ends into frosting to make basket handle. Store in tightly covered container.

makes 3 dozen cookies

edible easter baskets

festive easter cookies

1 cup butter, softened

2 cups powdered sugar

1 egg

2 teaspoons grated lemon peel

1 teaspoon vanilla

3 cups all-purpose flour

½ teaspoon salt

   Royal Icing (recipe follows)

   Assorted food colors

   Assorted sprinkles and candies

1 Beat butter and sugar in large bowl until fluffy. Add egg, lemon peel and vanilla; mix well. Combine flour and salt in medium bowl. Add to butter mixture; mix well. Divide dough in half. Wrap in plastic wrap. Chill 3 hours or overnight.

2 Preheat oven to 375°F. Roll dough on floured surface to ⅛-inch thickness. Cut out dough using Easter cookie cutters, such as eggs, bunnies and tulips. Place cutouts on ungreased cookie sheets.

3 Bake 8 to 12 minutes or just until edges are very lightly browned. Remove to wire racks; cool completely. Prepare Royal Icing; tint with food colors as desired. Decorate cookies as desired.

ROYAL ICING: Beat 1 room temperature egg white in small bowl with electric mixer at high speed until foamy. (Use only grade A clean, uncracked egg.) Gradually add 2 cups powdered sugar and ½ teaspoon almond extract. Beat at low speed until moistened. Increase mixer speed to high and beat until icing is stiff, adding up to ½ cup more powdered sugar if needed.

makes 4 dozen cookies

festive easter cookies

Summer fun

honey bees

¾ cup shortening

½ cup sugar

¼ cup honey

1 egg

½ teaspoon vanilla

2 cups all-purpose flour

⅓ cup cornmeal

1 teaspoon baking powder

½ teaspoon salt

**Yellow and black icings, gummy
fruit and decors**

1 Beat shortening, sugar and honey in large bowl at medium speed of electric mixer until fluffy. Add egg and vanilla; mix until well blended. Combine flour, cornmeal, baking powder and salt in medium bowl. Add to shortening mixture; mix at low speed until well blended. Wrap in plastic wrap; refrigerate 2 hours or overnight.

2 Preheat oven to 375°F. Divide dough into 24 equal sections. Shape each section into oval-shaped ball. Place 2 inches apart on ungreased cookie sheets.

3 Bake 10 to 12 minutes or until lightly browned. Cool 2 minutes on cookie sheets. Remove to wire racks; cool completely.

4 Decorate cookies with yellow and black icings, gummy fruit and decors as shown in photo to resemble honey bees.

makes 2 dozen cookies

honey bees

uncle sam's hat

1 package (about 18 ounces) refrigerated chocolate chip cookie dough

2 cups powdered sugar

2 to 4 tablespoons milk

Red and blue food colors

1 Preheat oven to 350°F. Lightly grease 12-inch round pizza pan and cookie sheet. Remove dough from wrapper. Press dough evenly into prepared pizza pan. Cut dough into hat shape as shown in photo. Press scraps together and flatten heaping tablespoonfuls of dough onto prepared cookie sheet. Using 1½- to 2-inch star cookie cutter, cut out several stars; remove and discard dough scraps.

2 Bake stars 5 to 7 minutes and hat 7 to 9 minutes or until lightly browned at edges. Cool stars on cookie sheet 1 minute. Remove to wire rack; cool completely. Cool hat completely on pan on rack.

3 Combine powdered sugar and enough milk, one tablespoon at a time, to make medium-thick pourable glaze. Spread small amount of glaze over stars and place on waxed paper; let stand until glaze is set. Using red and blue food colors, tint ½ of glaze red, tint ¼ of glaze blue and leave remaining ¼ of glaze white.

4 Decorate hat with red, white and blue glazes as shown in photo; place stars on blue band of hat. Let stand until glaze is set.

makes 1 large cookie

uncle sam's hat

rainbows

**Christmas Ornament Cookie
Dough (recipe follows)**

**Red, green, yellow and blue
paste food colors**

**White frosting and edible gold
glitter dust**

1 Prepare Christmas Ornament Cookie Dough as directed, but do not wrap and chill dough. Divide dough into 10 sections. Mix 4 sections dough and red food color until smooth. Mix 3 sections dough and green food color until smooth. Mix 2 sections dough and yellow food color until smooth. Combine remaining dough and blue food color until smooth. Wrap each dough section in plastic wrap. Chill 30 minutes.

2 Shape blue dough into 8-inch log. Shape yellow dough into 8×3-inch rectangle; place on waxed paper. Place blue log in center of yellow rectangle. Fold yellow edges up and around blue log; pinch to seal. Roll to form smooth log.

3 Roll green dough into 8×5-inch rectangle on waxed paper. Place yellow log in center of green rectangle. Fold green edges up and around yellow log; pinch to seal. Roll to form smooth log.

4 Roll red dough into 8×7-inch rectangle. Place green log in center of red rectangle. Fold red edges up and around green log; pinch to seal. Roll to form smooth log. Wrap in plastic wrap; refrigerate 1 hour.

makes 5 dozen cookies

rainbows

5 Preheat oven to 350°F. Grease cookie sheets. Cut log in half lengthwise. Cut each half into ¼-inch-thick slices. Place slices 1 inch apart on prepared cookie sheets. Bake 8 to 12 minutes. (Do not brown.) Cool on cookie sheets 1 minute. Remove to wire racks; cool completely.

6 Pipe small amount of frosting on bottom corner of 1 side of each cookie and sprinkle with glitter dust. Let stand 1 hour or until frosting sets.

CHRISTMAS ORNAMENT COOKIE DOUGH

1 cup sugar

¾ cup unsalted butter, softened

1 egg

1 teaspoon vanilla

1 teaspoon almond extract

2¼ cups all-purpose flour

¼ teaspoon salt

Beat sugar and butter until fluffy. Beat in egg, vanilla and almond extract. Beat in flour and salt until well blended. Form dough into 2 discs; wrap in plastic wrap and refrigerate 30 minutes or until firm.

cookie bowl and cookie fruit

1 cup butter, softened

1½ cups sugar

2 whole eggs

2 teaspoons grated orange peel

2 teaspoons vanilla

5 cups all-purpose flour

1 teaspoon baking powder

½ teaspoon salt

1 cup sour cream

4 egg yolks, divided

4 teaspoons water, divided

Red, yellow, blue and green liquid food colors

SUPPLIES

Small, clean craft paintbrushes

1 Beat butter and sugar in large bowl until fluffy. Beat in whole eggs, orange peel and vanilla until well blended. Mix flour, baking powder and salt. Stir half of flour mixture into butter mixture until blended. Add sour cream; mix well. Add remaining flour mixture; mix well. Divide dough into 4 sections. Wrap in plastic wrap; chill 2 hours.

2 Place 1 egg yolk in each of 4 separate bowls. Add 1 teaspoon water and food color to each; beat lightly. Set aside.

3 Preheat oven to 375°F. Roll 1 dough section on floured surface to 12-inch circle. Transfer to inverted 1½-quart ovenproof bowl. Press dough onto bowl; trim edges. Paint as desired using craft paintbrushes and egg yolk paints. Place on wire rack and then on cookie sheet. Bake 20 to 25 minutes or until browned. Cool on bowl.

4 Roll remaining dough on floured surface to ⅛-inch thickness. Cut with fruit-shaped cookie cutters. Place 2 inches apart on ungreased cookie sheets. Paint with egg yolk paints. Bake 10 to 12 minutes or until edges are browned. Remove to wire racks; cool completely.

makes 1 bowl and
4 dozen cookies

cookie bowl
and cookie fruit

baseball caps

I cup butter, softened

7 ounces almond paste

¾ cup sugar

I egg

I teaspoon vanilla

¼ teaspoon salt

3 cups all-purpose flour

Assorted colored icings and colored candies

1 Preheat oven to 350°F. Grease cookie sheets. Beat butter, almond paste, sugar, egg, vanilla and salt in large bowl until light and fluffy. Add flour all at once; stir just to combine.

2 Roll ¼ of dough on lightly floured surface to ⅛-inch thickness. Cut out I-inch circles. Place cutouts 2 inches apart on prepared cookie sheets.

3 Shape remaining dough into I-inch balls.* Place one ball on top of half dough circle so about ½ inch of circle sticks out to form bill of baseball cap. Repeat with remaining dough balls and circles.

4 Bake 10 to 12 minutes or until lightly browned. If bills brown too quickly, cut small strips of foil and cover with shiny side of foil facing up. Let cool on cookie sheets 2 minutes. Remove to wire racks; cool completely. Decorate with icings and candies as desired.

*Use a 1-tablespoon scoop to keep the baseball caps uniform in size.

makes 3 dozen cookies

baseball caps

high-flying flags

¾ **cup unsalted butter, softened**

¼ **cup granulated sugar**

¼ **cup packed light brown sugar**

1 **egg yolk**

1¾ **cups all-purpose flour**

¾ **teaspoon baking powder**

⅛ **teaspoon salt**

Lollipop sticks

Blue icing, white sugar stars, white icing and red string licorice

1 Combine butter, granulated sugar, brown sugar and egg yolk in medium bowl; mix until well blended. Add flour, baking powder and salt; mix until well blended. Wrap dough in plastic wrap and chill 1 hour or until firm.

2 Preheat oven to 350°F. Grease cookie sheets. Roll dough on lightly floured surface to ¼-inch thickness. Cut out dough using 3-inch flag-shaped cookie cutter. Place lollipop stick underneath left side of flag; press gently to adhere. Place flags 2 inches apart on prepared cookie sheets.

3 Bake 8 to 10 minutes or until edges are lightly browned. Remove to wire racks and cool completely.

4 Spread blue icing in square in upper left corner of each flag; place sugar stars on blue icing. Spread white icing over plain sections of remaining cookies. Place strips of red licorice on white icing; let set.

makes 3 dozen cookies

lady bugs

¾ **cup shortening**

½ **cup sugar**

¼ **cup honey**

 1 **egg**

½ **teaspoon vanilla**

 2 **cups all-purpose flour**

⅓ **cup cornmeal**

 1 **teaspoon baking powder**

½ **teaspoon salt**

   **Orange and black icings and
   yellow candy-coated pieces**

1 Beat shortening, sugar and honey in large bowl at medium speed with electric mixer until light and fluffy. Add egg and vanilla; mix until well blended. Combine flour, cornmeal, baking powder and salt in medium bowl. Add to shortening mixture; mix at low speed until blended. Wrap dough in plastic wrap; chill 2 hours or overnight.

2 Preheat oven to 375°F. Divide dough into 24 equal sections. Shape each section into 2×1¼-inch oval-shaped ball. Place balls 2 inches apart on ungreased cookie sheets.

3 Bake 10 to 12 minutes or until lightly browned. Cool on cookie sheets 2 minutes. Remove to wire racks; cool completely.

4 Decorate cookies with orange and black icings and candy-coated pieces as shown in photo to resemble lady bugs.

makes 2 dozen cookies

lady bugs

sunshine butter cookies

¾ **cup butter, softened**

¾ **cup sugar**

1 **egg**

2¼ **cups all-purpose flour**

¼ **teaspoon salt**

Grated peel of ½ lemon

1 **teaspoon frozen lemonade concentrate, thawed**

Lemonade Royal Icing (recipe follows)

Thin pretzel sticks

Gummy fruit and black licorice strings

1 Beat butter and sugar until fluffy. Add egg; beat well. Stir in flour, salt and lemon peel. Stir in concentrate. Wrap in plastic wrap; chill 2 hours.

2 Preheat oven to 350°F. Grease cookie sheets. Roll dough on floured surface to ⅛-inch thickness. Cut dough using 3-inch round cutter. Place cutouts on prepared cookie sheets. Press pretzel sticks into cutouts for sunshine rays. Bake 10 minutes or until browned. Remove to wire racks; cool completely.

3 Prepare Lemonade Royal Icing. Spoon ½ cup icing into resealable plastic food storage bag; seal. Cut tiny corner from bag. Pipe outline at edge of flat side of each cookie. Add water, 1 tablespoon at a time, to remaining icing in bowl until thick but pourable consistency. Spoon icing into centers, staying within outline. Decorate faces as desired. Let set.

LEMONADE ROYAL ICING: Beat 3¾ cups powdered sugar, 6 tablespoons thawed frozen lemonade concentrate and 3 tablespoons meringue powder at high speed of electric mixer until smooth. Tint with yellow food color.

makes 3 dozen cookies

sunshine butter cookies

rollerblade cookies

½ cup butter, softened

1¼ cups honey

1 cup packed brown sugar

1 egg yolk

5½ cups self-rising flour

1 teaspoon ground ginger

1 teaspoon ground cinnamon

½ cup milk

1 egg white, beaten

1 tablespoon cold water

Toasted oats cereal

Assorted colored icings, colored sugars and colored sprinkles

1. Beat butter, honey, sugar and egg yolk in large bowl at medium speed of electric mixer until light and fluffy. Combine flour, ginger and cinnamon in small bowl; add alternately with milk to butter mixture. Beat just until combined. Cover; refrigerate 30 minutes.

2. Preheat oven to 350°F. Grease cookie sheets. Roll dough on lightly floured surface to ¼-inch thickness. Cut out cookies using 3½-inch boot-shaped cookie cutter. Place 2 inches apart on prepared cookie sheets.

3. Beat egg white and water in small bowl until combined. Lightly brush bottom of each boot with egg white mixture. Place 6 toasted oats on bottom of each boot for wheels.

4. Bake 8 to 10 minutes or until lightly browned. Cool 2 minutes on cookie sheet. Remove to wire rack; cool completely.

5. Decorate cookies with colored icings, colored sugars and sprinkles as desired to resemble rollerblades.

makes 4 dozen cookies

hot dog cookies

Butter Cookie Dough (page 87)

Liquid food colors

Sesame seeds

Shredded coconut, red and green decorator gels, frosting and gummy candies

1 Prepare and chill Butter Cookie Dough as directed. Lightly grease cookie sheets.

2 To make "hot dogs," use $1/3$ of dough, keeping remaining dough in refrigerator. Mix food colors in small bowl to get reddish-brown color following chart on back of food color box. Mix color evenly into reserved dough. Divide colored dough into 6 equal sections. Roll each section into thin log shape. Round edges; set aside.

3 To make "buns," divide remaining dough into 6 equal sections. Roll sections into thick logs. Make very deep indentation the length of logs in centers; smooth edges. Dip sides in sesame seeds. Place 3 inches apart on prepared cookie sheets. Place hot dogs inside buns. Freeze 20 minutes.

4 Preheat oven to 350°F. Bake 17 to 20 minutes or until bun edges are light golden brown. Cool completely on cookie sheets.

5 Top hot dogs with green-tinted coconut for "relish," white coconut for "onions," red decorator gel for "ketchup" and yellow-tinted frosting or whipped topping for "mustard."

makes 6 large cookies

hot dog cookies

Autumn delights

autumn leaves

1½ cups unsalted butter, softened

⅔ cup packed light brown sugar

1 egg

½ teaspoon vanilla

3 cups all-purpose flour

1 teaspoon ground cinnamon

½ teaspoon salt

⅛ teaspoon ground ginger

⅛ teaspoon ground cloves

2 tablespoons unsweetened cocoa powder

Yellow, orange and red food colors

¼ cup semisweet chocolate chips, melted

1 Beat butter and brown sugar in large bowl until fluffy. Beat in egg and vanilla. Add flour, cinnamon, salt, ginger and cloves; beat until well blended.

2 Divide dough into 5 equal sections; reserve 1 section. Stir cocoa into 1 section until well blended. Stir yellow food color into 1 section until well blended. Repeat with remaining 2 sections and orange and red food colors.

3 Preheat oven to 350°F. Grease cookie sheets. Working with half of each dough color, press colors together lightly. Roll out dough on floured surface to ¼-inch thickness. Cut dough with leaf-shaped cookie cutters of various shapes and sizes. Place 2 inches apart on prepared cookie sheets. Repeat with remaining dough and scraps. Bake 10 to 15 minutes or until edges are lightly browned. Remove to wire racks; cool completely.

4 Place melted chocolate in resealable plastic food storage bag. Cut off very tiny corner of bag. Pipe chocolate onto cookies in vein patterns.

makes 1½ dozen cookies

autumn leaves

nutty footballs

1 cup butter, softened

½ cup sugar

1 egg

½ teaspoon vanilla

2 cups all-purpose flour

¼ cup unsweetened cocoa powder

1 cup finely chopped almonds

Colored icings (optional)

White icing

1 Beat butter and sugar in large bowl until creamy. Add egg and vanilla; mix until well blended. Stir together flour and cocoa; gradually add to butter mixture, beating until well blended. Add almonds; beat until well blended. Shape dough into disc. Wrap dough in plastic wrap; chill 30 minutes.

2 Preheat oven to 350°F. Lightly grease cookie sheets. Roll out dough on floured surface to ¼-inch thickness. Cut dough with 2½- to 3-inch football-shaped cookie cutter.* Place 2 inches apart on prepared cookie sheets.

3 Bake 10 to 12 minutes or until set. Cool on cookie sheets 1 to 2 minutes. Remove to wire racks; cool completely. Decorate with colored icings, if desired. Pipe white icing onto footballs to make laces.

*If you do not have a football-shaped cookie cutter, create a pattern following the directions on page 5. Or, shape 3 tablespoonfuls of dough into oval. Place 3 inches apart on prepared cookie sheets. Flatten ovals to ¼-inch thickness; taper ends. Bake as directed.

makes 2 dozen cookies

nutty footballs

black cat cookies

1 package (18 ounces)
    refrigerated sugar cookie
    dough

All-purpose flour (optional)

White Decorator Frosting
    (recipe follows)

Black paste food color

Assorted colored candies

1 Preheat oven to 350°F. Remove dough from wrapper. Divide dough in half. Reserve 1 half; cover and refrigerate remaining half.

2 Roll reserved dough on lightly floured surface to ⅛-inch thickness. Sprinkle with flour to minimize sticking, if necessary.

3 Cut dough using 3½-inch cat face cookie cutter. Place cutouts 2 inches apart on ungreased baking sheets. Repeat with remaining dough and scraps.

4 Bake 8 to 10 minutes or until firm but not browned. Cool on baking sheets 2 minutes. Remove to wire racks; cool completely.

5 Prepare White Decorator Frosting. Add desired amount of food color to make black. Decorate cookies with frosting and assorted candies as desired to make cat faces.

WHITE DECORATOR FROSTING: Combine 1 pound powdered sugar, ½ cup vegetable shortening, 1 tablespoon corn syrup and 6 tablespoons milk in bowl. Beat 2 minutes or until fluffy, adding additional milk if necessary.

makes about 20 cookies

black cat cookies

candy corn cookies

**Butter Cookie Dough
(page 87)**

Cookie Glaze (recipe follows)

Yellow and orange food colors

1 Prepare and chill Butter Cookie Dough as directed.

2 Preheat oven to 350°F. Roll dough on floured surface to ¼-inch thickness. Cut out 3-inch candy corn shapes from dough. Place cutouts on ungreased cookie sheets.

3 Bake 8 to 10 minutes or until edges are lightly browned. Remove to wire racks to cool completely. Prepare Cookie Glaze.

4 Place racks over waxed-paper-lined baking sheets. Divide Cookie Glaze into thirds; place in separate small bowls. Tint ⅓ glaze with yellow food color and ⅓ with orange food color. Leave remaining glaze white. Spoon glazes over cookies to resemble candy corn as shown in photo. Let stand until glaze is set.

COOKIE GLAZE: Combine 4 cups powdered sugar and 4 tablespoons milk in small bowl. Add 1 to 2 tablespoons more milk as needed to make medium-thick, pourable glaze.

makes 2 dozen cookies

candy corn cookies
and bat cookie

BAT COOKIES: Omit yellow and orange food colors. Prepare recipe as directed except use bat cookie cutter to cut out dough. Bake as directed. Tint glaze with black paste food color; spoon over cookies. Decorate with decors and sprinkles as desired.

sweet spiders

1 package (18 ounces) refrigerated sugar cookie dough

¼ cup unsweetened cocoa powder

3 to 4 tablespoons seedless red raspberry or cherry preserves*

Chocolate licorice

Decors, cinnamon candies, assorted icings, sprinkles and mini chocolate chips

If there are large pieces of fruit in preserves, purée in food processor until smooth.

1. Preheat oven to 350°F. Grease cookie sheets; set aside. Remove dough from wrapper. Combine dough and cocoa in large bowl; mix until well blended.

2. Evenly divide dough into 20 pieces. Shape each piece into 2 (1-inch) balls and 1 (½-inch) ball. For each spider body, flatten 1 (1-inch) ball into 2-inch circle on prepared cookie sheet. Place ½ teaspoon preserves in center of circle. Flatten remaining 1-inch ball into 2-inch circle and place over preserves, sealing dough edges. Cut licorice into 1½-inch pieces; cut pieces in half lengthwise. Press licorice into spider body for legs.

3. For each spider head, slightly flatten ½-inch ball and lightly press into spider body. Press decors or cinnamon candies into head for eyes.

4. Bake 10 to 12 minutes or until cookies are set. Cool on cookie sheets 10 minutes; transfer to wire racks to cool completely. Decorate as desired with assorted icings, decors, sprinkles and mini chocolate chips.

makes 20 cookies

sweet spiders

coffin cookies

I package (18 ounces) refrigerated chocolate cookie dough*

All-purpose flour (optional)

Marshmallow Filling (recipe follows)

Colored sprinkles and sugars, prepared white icing and Halloween decors

If refrigerated chocolate cookie dough is unavailable, add ¼ cup unsweetened cocoa powder to refrigerated sugar cookie dough. Beat in large bowl until well blended.

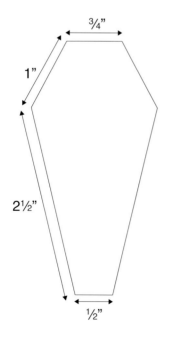

¾"

1"

2½"

½"

1 Draw pattern for coffin on cardboard following diagram; cut out pattern. Preheat oven to 350°F. Remove dough from wrapper. Cut dough in half. Wrap one dough half in plastic wrap; refrigerate.

2 Roll remaining dough on lightly floured surface to ⅛-inch thickness. Sprinkle with flour to minimize sticking, if necessary. Place pattern on cookie dough; cut dough around pattern with sharp knife. Repeat as necessary. Place cutouts 2 inches apart on ungreased baking sheets. Repeat with remaining dough and scraps.

3 Bake about 6 minutes or until firm but not browned. Cool on baking sheets 2 minutes. Remove to wire racks; cool completely.

4 Prepare Marshmallow Filling. Spread half of cookies with 2 teaspoons filling each; top with remaining cookies. Roll cookie sandwich edges in sprinkles. Decorate as desired.

MARSHMALLOW FILLING: In small bowl, combine 1 cup prepared vanilla frosting with ¾ cup marshmallow creme until well blended.

makes about 2 dozen
sandwich cookies

coffin cookies

creepy cookie cauldrons

1 package (18 ounces) refrigerated chocolate cookie dough*

All-purpose flour (optional)

1 bag (14 ounces) caramels, unwrapped

2 tablespoons milk

1 cup crisp rice cereal

¼ cup mini candy-coated chocolate pieces

Black licorice whips and small gummy insects, frogs or lizards

*If refrigerated chocolate cookie dough is unavailable, add ¼ cup unsweetened cocoa powder to refrigerated sugar cookie dough. Beat in large bowl until well blended.

1 Grease 36 (1¾-inch) mini muffin cups. Remove dough from wrapper. Sprinkle dough with flour to minimize sticking, if necessary. Cut dough into 36 equal pieces; roll into balls. Place 1 ball in bottom of each muffin cup. Press dough on bottoms and up sides of muffin cups; chill 15 minutes. Preheat oven to 350°F.

2 Bake 8 to 9 minutes. (Cookies will be puffy.) Remove from oven; gently press down center of each cookie. Return to oven 1 minute. Cool cookies in muffin cups 5 minutes. Remove to wire racks; cool completely.

3 Melt caramels and milk in small saucepan over low heat, stirring frequently until smooth. Stir in cereal. Spoon 1 heaping teaspoon caramel mixture into each cookie cup. Immediately sprinkle with mini chocolate pieces.

4 Cut licorice whips into 4½-inch lengths. For each cookie, make small slit in side; insert end of licorice strip. Repeat on other side of cookie to make cauldron handle. Decorate with gummy creatures as desired.

makes 3 dozen cookies

creepy cookie cauldrons

thanksgiving day place cards

8 marshmallow puff cookies

4 striped shortbread ring cookies

¼ cup semisweet chocolate chips, melted

8 pieces candy corn

8 ice cream sugar cones

3 ounces semisweet chocolate, melted

Assorted fall candies

SUPPLIES

8 (2½ × 1½-inch) pieces lightweight cardboard

8 (2 × ¾-inch) pieces lightweight cardboard

1 Cut down into marshmallow cookie halfway between center and edge. Starting in back, cut horizontally toward first cut. Dip knife in hot water and dry it before each cut. Discard pieces.

2 Cut striped cookies in half. Attach 1 striped cookie half with melted chocolate to cut edge of marshmallow cookie to form turkey tail. Attach candy corn to front of turkey with melted chocolate as shown. Repeat with remaining cookies.

3 To make place cards, write names near top edges of large cardboard rectangles. Place behind striped cookie half. Attach rectangle with melted chocolate, if desired; let set.

4 Dip edges of sugar cones into melted chocolate; let stand on wire racks or waxed paper until chocolate is set. Place each cone on its side; fill with candy.

5 To make place cards, write names on small cardboard rectangles. Attach to tops of cones with melted chocolate, if desired; let set.

makes 16 place cards

thanksgiving day place cards

Winter treasures

icicle ornaments

2½ cups all-purpose flour

¼ teaspoon salt

1 cup sugar

¾ cup unsalted butter, softened

2 squares (1 ounce each) white
   chocolate, melted

1 egg

1 teaspoon vanilla

Coarse white decorating sugar,
   colored sugars and decors

SUPPLIES
Ribbon

1 Combine flour and salt in medium bowl. Beat sugar and butter in large bowl at medium speed of electric mixer until fluffy. Beat in melted white chocolate, egg and vanilla. Gradually add flour mixture. Beat at low speed until well blended. Shape into disc. Wrap dough in plastic wrap and refrigerate 30 minutes or until firm.

2 Preheat oven to 350°F. Grease cookie sheets. Shape heaping tablespoonfuls of dough into 10-inch ropes. Fold each rope in half; twist to make icicle shape, leaving opening at top and tapering ends. Roll in coarse sugar; sprinkle with colored sugars and decors as desired. Place 1 inch apart on prepared cookie sheets.

3 Bake 8 to 10 minutes. (Do not brown.) Cool on cookie sheets 1 minute. Remove to wire racks; cool completely. Pull ribbon through opening in top of each icicle; tie small knot in ribbon ends.

makes 2½ dozen cookies

icicle ornaments

fireside cookie

1 package (18 ounces) refrigerated cookie dough, any flavor

All-purpose flour (optional)

Icings, red licorice bites, black string licorice, gumdrops and assorted candies

1 Preheat oven to 350°F. Line large baking sheets with parchment paper. Remove dough from wrapper. Using about $\frac{1}{4}$ of dough, roll into 12×3-inch strip. Trim to 11×2$\frac{1}{4}$ inches; set aside. Roll remaining dough into 10×8-inch rectangle. Trim to 9×7$\frac{3}{4}$ inches; place on prepared baking sheet. Place reserved dough strip at top of rectangle to make fireplace mantel. Roll remaining scraps and cut into stocking shapes. Place on prepared baking sheets.

2 Bake 10 minutes or until edges are lightly browned. Cool on baking sheets 5 minutes. Remove stocking cookies to wire rack. Slide large cookie and parchment paper onto wire rack; cool completely.

3 Decorate with icings and assorted candies as shown in photo, attaching stockings to fireplace cookie with icing.

makes 1 large cookie

fireside cookie

star cookie christmas tree

COOKIE DOUGH

2¾ cups flour

1 teaspoon ground ginger

½ teaspoon ground cinnamon

¼ teaspoon salt

⅔ cup KARO® Light Corn Syrup

½ cup packed brown sugar

6 tablespoons margarine

ICING

¼ cup (½ stick) margarine

3 tablespoons KARO® Light Corn Syrup

1½ cups confectioners' sugar

2 teaspoons milk

1 teaspoon vanilla

Green food color

Green crystal sugar and yellow crystal sugar

Miniature colored candies

SUPPLIES

One 10-inch wooden dowel or chopstick (about ¼-inch in diameter)

One 3- or 4-inch styrofoam ball for base

1 FOR COOKIE DOUGH: In large bowl, stir flour, ginger, cinnamon and salt. In 1-quart saucepan, combine corn syrup, brown sugar and margarine; stir over medium heat until margarine is melted. Stir into flour mixture until well blended. On waxed paper, press dough into rectangle; divide in half. (Do not refrigerate dough before rolling.)

2 Preheat oven to 350°F. On foil-lined baking sheets roll each dough half to scant ¼ inch thick. With set of ten graduated star-shaped cookie cutters, cut dough into 10 graduated stars. Using smallest cutter, cut 9 more cookies to use as spacers. Remove dough trimmings and reroll. Arrange stars on ungreased cookie sheets.

3 Bake 10 to 15 minutes or until lightly browned. While cookies are warm, use dowel to make center hole in each cookie. Cool on wire racks.

4 FOR ICING: In small bowl with mixer at medium speed, beat margarine, corn syrup, confectioners' sugar, milk and vanilla until smooth. Reserve about 2 tablespoons icing. Tint remaining icing with green food color.

makes 1 centerpiece

star cookie christmas tree

5 FOR BASE: Cut 1-inch-thick center slice from styrofoam ball. Insert wooden dowel upright in center of slice.

6 TO ASSEMBLE TREE: Starting with largest cookie, spread stars with frosting and sprinkle with green sugar. Slide star down dowel; top with one unfrosted spacer cookie. Repeat with remaining cookies, stacking on dowel in descending size. Sandwich two small stars together; spread with reserved white icing and sprinkle with yellow sugar. Place on edge to form top star. Decorate as desired with candies.

stained glass cookies

½ cup margarine or butter, softened

½ cup sugar

½ cup honey

1 egg

1 teaspoon vanilla extract

3 cups all-purpose flour

1 teaspoon DAVIS® Baking Powder

½ teaspoon baking soda

½ teaspoon salt

5 (1.14-ounce) rolls LIFE SAVERS® Five Flavor Roll Candy

1 Beat margarine or butter, sugar, honey, egg and vanilla in large bowl with electric mixer until creamy. Mix in flour, baking powder, baking soda and salt. Cover; refrigerate at least 2 hours.

2 Roll dough on lightly floured surface to ¼-inch thickness. Cut dough into desired shapes with 2½- to 3-inch floured cookie cutters. Trace smaller version of cookie shape on dough leaving ½- to ¾-inch border of dough. Cut out and remove dough from center of cookies; set aside. Place cut-out shapes on baking sheets lined with foil. Repeat with reserved dough, re-rolling scraps as necessary.

3 Crush each color of candy separately between two layers of wax paper with a mallet. Spoon crushed candy inside centers of cut-out cookie shapes (about ½ teaspoon for each cookie).

4 Bake at 350°F for 6 to 8 minutes or until candy is melted and cookies are lightly browned. Cool cookies completely before removing from foil.

makes 3½ dozen cookies

stained glass cookies

angels

**Butter Cookie Dough
(page 87)**

1 egg, lightly beaten

**Small pretzels, white frosting,
shredded coconut, edible
glitter dust and assorted
small decors**

1 Prepare and chill Butter Cookie Dough as directed.

2 Preheat oven to 350°F. Grease cookie sheets. Roll dough on floured surface to ¼-inch thickness. Cut out 12 (4-inch) triangles. Reroll scraps to ¼-inch thickness. Cut out 12 (1½-inch) circles.

3 Place triangles on prepared cookie sheets. Brush with beaten egg. Attach circle, pressing gently. Bake 8 to 10 minutes or just until edges begin to brown. Remove to wire racks; cool completely.

4 Attach pretzels to back of each cookie for wings using frosting as "glue." Let stand 30 minutes or until frosting is set. Pipe frosting around hairline of each angel; sprinkle with coconut and glitter dust.

5 Decorate cookies with frosting, coconut, glitter dust and decors to resemble angels as shown in photo or as desired. Let cookies stand until frosting is set.

makes 1 dozen cookies

angels

hanukkah cookies

½ cup unsalted butter, softened

1 package (3 ounces) cream cheese

½ cup sugar

¼ cup honey

1 egg

½ teaspoon vanilla

2½ cups all-purpose flour

⅓ cup finely ground walnuts

1 teaspoon baking powder

¼ teaspoon salt

Assorted colored icings

1 Beat butter, cream cheese, sugar, honey, egg and vanilla in large bowl at medium speed of electric mixer until creamy. Stir in flour, walnuts, baking powder and salt until well blended. Form dough into ball; wrap in plastic wrap and flatten. Refrigerate about 2 hours or until firm.

2 Preheat oven to 350°F. Lightly grease cookie sheets. Roll out dough, small portion at a time, to ¼-inch thickness on floured surface with lightly floured rolling pin. (Keep remaining dough wrapped in refrigerator.) Cut out dough with 2½- to 3-inch dreidel-shaped cookie cutter and 6-pointed star cookie cutter. Transfer to prepared cookie sheets.

3 Bake 8 to 10 minutes or until edges are lightly browned. Let cookies stand on cookie sheets 1 to 2 minutes; transfer to wire racks to cool completely. Decorate cookies with colored icings as desired.

makes 3½ dozen cookies

hanukkah cookies

philadelphia®
snowmen cookies

1 package (8 ounces)
   **PHILADELPHIA® Cream
   Cheese, softened**

1 cup powdered sugar

¾ cup (1½ sticks) butter *or*
   margarine

½ teaspoon vanilla

2¼ cups flour

½ teaspoon baking soda

   Sifted powdered sugar

   **Miniature peanut butter cups
   (optional)**

MIX cream cheese, 1 cup sugar, butter and vanilla with electric mixer on medium speed until well blended. Add flour and baking soda; mix well.

SHAPE dough into equal number of ½-inch and 1-inch diameter balls. Using 1 small and 1 large ball for each snowman, place balls, slightly overlapping, on ungreased cookie sheets. Flatten to ¼-inch thickness with bottom of glass dipped in additional flour. Repeat with remaining balls.

BAKE at 325°F for 19 to 21 minutes or until light golden brown. Cool on wire racks. Sprinkle each snowman with sifted powdered sugar. Decorate with icing as desired. Cut peanut butter cups in half for hats.

makes about
3 dozen cookies

philadelphia®
snowmen cookies

valentine's day cookie cards

Butter Cookie Dough (recipe follows)

1 container (16 ounces) vanilla frosting

1 container (16 ounces) pink cherry-flavored frosting

Assorted candies

SUPPLIES

Pastry bags and assorted decorating tips

1 Preheat oven to 350°F. Lightly grease cookie sheets. On lightly floured surface, roll dough ⅛-inch-thick. Cut out 4½×3-inch rectangles; place on cookie sheets.

2 Bake rectangles 8 to 10 minutes or until edges are lightly browned. Remove to wire racks and let cool completely.

3 Spread cookies with frostings as desired; spoon remaining frostings into pastry bags fitted with decorating tips. Decorate with frostings and candies to resemble Valentine's Day cards.

makes 1 dozen cookies

valentine's day
cookie cards

BUTTER COOKIE DOUGH

1¾ cups all-purpose flour

¾ teaspoon baking powder

⅛ teaspoon salt

1 cup butter, softened

¼ cup each granulated sugar and packed light brown sugar

1 egg yolk

Combine flour, baking powder and salt in small bowl; set aside. Combine butter, granulated sugar and brown sugar in medium bowl; beat at high speed of electric mixer until fluffy. Beat in egg yolk until well blended. Stir flour mixture into butter mixture until well blended. Wrap dough in plastic wrap; refrigerate 4 hours or until firm.

chocolate and peanut butter hearts

Chocolate Cookie Dough (recipe follows)

½ **cup shortening**

½ **cup creamy peanut butter**

1 **cup sugar**

1 **egg**

3 **tablespoons milk**

1 **teaspoon vanilla**

2 **cups all-purpose flour**

1 **teaspoon baking powder**

¼ **teaspoon salt**

1 Prepare and chill Chocolate Cookie Dough as directed.

2 Beat shortening, peanut butter and sugar until fluffy. Add egg, milk and vanilla; mix well. Combine flour, baking powder and salt. Beat flour mixture into peanut butter mixture until well blended. Wrap dough in plastic wrap. Refrigerate 1 to 2 hours or until firm.

3 Preheat oven to 350°F. Grease cookie sheets. Roll peanut butter dough on floured waxed paper to ⅛-inch thickness. Cut dough using 3-inch heart-shaped cookie cutter. Place cutouts on prepared cookie sheets. Repeat with chocolate dough.

4 Use smaller heart-shaped cookie cutter to remove small section from centers of hearts. Place small peanut butter hearts into large chocolate hearts; place small chocolate hearts into large peanut butter hearts. Press together lightly. Bake 12 to 14 minutes or until edges are browned. Remove to wire racks; cool.

makes 4 dozen cookies

chocolate and peanut butter hearts

CHOCOLATE COOKIE DOUGH

$2\frac{1}{4}$ cups all-purpose flour

1 teaspoon baking powder

$\frac{1}{4}$ teaspoon salt

1 cup butter, softened

1 cup sugar

1 egg

1 teaspoon vanilla

2 ounces semisweet chocolate, melted

Combine flour, baking powder and salt in small bowl; set aside. Combine butter and sugar in large bowl; beat at high speed of electric mixer until light and fluffy. Beat in egg and vanilla until well blended. Add melted chocolate; mix well. Stir flour mixture into butter mixture until well blended. Wrap dough in plastic wrap; refrigerate about 2 hours or until firm.

chocolate x and o cookies

⅔ **cup butter or margarine, softened**

1 **cup sugar**

2 **teaspoons vanilla extract**

2 **eggs**

2 **tablespoons light corn syrup**

2½ **cups all-purpose flour**

½ **cup HERSHEY᾽S Cocoa**

½ **teaspoon baking soda**

¼ **teaspoon salt**

    Decorating icing

1 Beat butter, sugar and vanilla in large bowl on medium speed of mixer until fluffy. Add eggs; beat well. Beat in corn syrup.

2 Combine flour, cocoa, baking soda and salt; gradually add to butter mixture, beating until well blended. Cover; refrigerate until dough is firm enough to handle.

3 Heat oven to 350°F. Shape dough into X and O shapes.* Place on ungreased cookie sheet.

4 Bake 5 minutes or until set. Remove from cookie sheet to wire rack. Cool completely. Decorate as desired with icing.

*To shape X's: Shape rounded teaspoons of dough into 3-inch logs. Place 1 log on cookie sheet; press lightly in center. Place another 3-inch log on top of first one, forming X shape. To shape O's: Shape rounded teaspoons dough into 5-inch logs. Connect ends, pressing lightly, forming O shape.

makes about
5 dozen cookies

chocolate x and o cookies

Special occasions

wedding bells

I cup unsalted butter, softened

¾ cup sugar

2 eggs

2½ cups all-purpose flour

I teaspoon baking powder

¼ teaspoon salt

¼ teaspoon ground cinnamon

Assorted icings, colored
sprinkles, sugars and decors

SUPPLIES

Thin ribbon

1. Beat butter and sugar in large bowl at medium speed of electric mixer until creamy. Add eggs; beat until fluffy. Stir in flour, baking powder, salt and cinnamon until well blended. Form dough into ball; wrap in plastic wrap and flatten. Refrigerate 2 hours or until firm.

2. Preheat oven to 350°F. Lightly grease cookie sheets. Roll out dough, small portion at a time, to ¼-inch thickness on floured surface with lightly floured rolling pin. (Keep remaining dough wrapped in refrigerator.) Cut out dough with 2½-inch bell-shaped cookie cutter. Transfer to prepared cookie sheets. Make small hole in top of each bell.

3. Bake 10 to 12 minutes or until edges are lightly browned. Let cookies stand on cookie sheets I minute; transfer to wire racks to cool completely. Decorate cookies with icings, sprinkles, sugars and decors to match wedding colors. Tie 2 bells together with ribbon.

makes 3 dozen cookies

wedding bells

abc blocks

2 recipes Christmas Ornament Cookie Dough (recipe follows)

Red food color

1 Prepare 2 recipes Christmas Ornament Cookie Dough as directed, but do not chill. Tint one recipe dough to desired shade of red with food color. Wrap doughs separately in plastic wrap and refrigerate 30 minutes.

2 Shape ⅔ red dough into 1½×1½×6-inch square log, pressing log on sides to flatten. Shape ⅔ plain dough into 1½×1½×6-inch square log, pressing log on sides to flatten.

3 Roll remaining ⅓ red dough into 6×7-inch rectangle on waxed paper. Place plain log in center of red rectangle. Fold red edges up and around plain log. Press gently on top and sides of dough so entire log is wrapped in red dough. Flatten log slightly to form square log. Roll remaining ⅓ plain dough into 6×7-inch rectangle on waxed paper. Place red log in center of plain rectangle. Fold plain edges up and around red log. Press gently on top and sides of dough so entire log is wrapped in plain dough. Flatten log slightly to form square log. Wrap each log in plastic wrap and refrigerate 1 hour.

makes 3 dozen cookies

abc blocks

4 Preheat oven to 350°F. Grease cookie sheets. Cut each log into same number of 1/4-inch-thick slices. Place slices 1 inch apart on prepared cookie sheets. Using 1 1/2-inch cookie cutters, cut out letter shapes from blocks, making sure to cut same number of each letter from red and plain dough. Place red letters in plain blocks and plain letters in red blocks; press lightly.

5 Bake 8 to 10 minutes. (Do not brown.) Cool on cookie sheets 1 minute. Remove to wire racks; cool completely.

CHRISTMAS ORNAMENT COOKIE DOUGH

3/4 cup unsalted butter, softened

1 cup sugar

1 egg

1 teaspoon *each* vanilla and almond extract

2 1/4 cups all-purpose flour

1/4 teaspoon salt

Beat butter and sugar until fluffy. Beat in egg, vanilla and almond extract. Beat in flour and salt until well blended. Form dough into 2 discs; wrap in plastic wrap and chill 30 minutes or until firm.

baby bottles

¾ **cup unsalted butter, softened**

¾ **cup sugar**

1 **egg**

1 **teaspoon vanilla**

1½ **cups cake flour**

1 **cup all-purpose flour**

¾ **teaspoon baking powder**

White, pink and blue icings

1. Beat butter, sugar, egg and vanilla in large bowl until creamy. Stir in flours and baking powder until well blended. Form dough into ball; wrap in plastic wrap and flatten. Refrigerate about 2 hours or until firm. Draw pattern for bottle on cardboard following diagram; cut out pattern.

2. Preheat oven to 350°F. Lightly grease cookie sheets. Roll dough to ¼-inch thickness on floured surface. Place pattern on cookie dough; cut dough around pattern with sharp knife. Repeat with remaining dough and scraps. Place cutouts 2 inches apart on ungreased baking sheets.

3. Bake cutouts 8 to 10 minutes or until edges are golden. Cool on cookie sheets 1 to 2 minutes. Remove to wire racks to cool completely.

4. Decorate cookies with white, pink and blue icings as shown in photo or as desired. Let stand until icing is set.

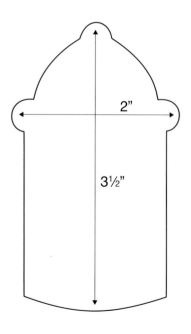

2"

3½"

makes 2 dozen cookies

baby bottles

congrats grad!

1 package (20 ounces) refrigerated sugar cookie dough

¼ cup all-purpose flour

¼ cup creamy peanut butter

1 cup mini chocolate chips

Granulated sugar

Small gumdrops to match school colors

Cookie Glaze (recipe follows)

Food colors to match school colors

12 graham cracker squares

1. Preheat oven to 350°F. Grease 12 (2½-inch) muffin cups. Remove dough from wrapper. Combine cookie dough, flour and peanut butter in large bowl until well mixed. Stir in chocolate chips. Divide dough into 12 equal pieces. Press each dough piece onto bottom and up side of each muffin cup.

2. Bake 15 to 18 minutes or until lightly browned; let cool in pan on wire rack 10 minutes. Remove from pan and cool completely on wire rack.

3. Sprinkle sugar on cutting board. For tassels, slightly flatten 3 gumdrops. Place gumdrops, with ends overlapping slightly, on sugared surface. Sprinkle with additional sugar. Roll flattened gumdrops into 3×1-inch piece with rolling pin, turning piece over frequently to coat with sugar. Trim and discard edges of gumdrop piece. Cut piece into 2½×¼-inch strips. Cut bottom part into several lengthwise strips to form fringe.

makes 1 dozen
large cookies

congrats grad!

4 Prepare Cookie Glaze. Tint glaze desired color. Place cookies upside down on wire racks set over waxed paper. Spread glaze over cookies to cover completely. Spread glaze over graham crackers; carefully set crackers on tops of cookies. Place tassel on each cap. Set gumdrop in center of each graham cracker for cap button. Let stand 40 minutes or until glaze is set.

COOKIE GLAZE: Combine 4 cups powdered sugar and 6 to 8 tablespoons milk, I tablespoon at a time, to make a medium-thick pourable glaze.

mini wedding cakes

1½ cups all-purpose flour

1 teaspoon baking powder

½ teaspoon salt

½ cup unsalted butter, softened

¾ cup granulated sugar

¾ cup packed light brown sugar

2 eggs

2 teaspoons vanilla

White Glaze (recipe follows)

Royal Icing (page 34)

Assorted colored decors

SUPPLIES

Pastry bags and assorted
decorating tips

1 Preheat oven to 350°F. Grease 15×10-inch jelly-roll pan; set aside. Mix flour, baking powder and salt in small bowl; set aside. Beat butter and sugars in large bowl until fluffy. Beat in eggs and vanilla. Add flour mixture. Beat until well blended. Spread batter evenly in prepared pan. Bake 15 to 20 minutes or until golden brown. Remove pan to wire rack; cool completely.

2 Using 2¾-inch, 2-inch and ¾-inch round cutters, cut 8 circles of each size. Prepare White Glaze. Spread some glaze on tops of large and medium circles. Place medium circles on large circles; place small circles on medium circles. Let set.

3 Place cookies on wire racks set over waxed paper. Spread glaze over cookies to cover. Decorate as desired with Royal Icing and decors. Let set.

WHITE GLAZE: Mix 4 cups powdered sugar, 6 tablespoons water and 3 tablespoons meringue powder at high speed of electric mixer for 6 to 7 minutes to make a medium-thick pourable glaze. (*Meringue powder is a dried egg-white-based powder. It can be found in the cake decorating section of most craft stores.*)

makes about
10 large cookies

mini wedding cakes

sweet showers

I cup unsalted butter, softened

½ cup sugar

I teaspoon lemon extract

I teaspoon orange extract

½ teaspoon vanilla

2½ cups all-purpose flour

⅛ teaspoon salt

Assorted icings, colored sprinkles, sugars and decors

1. Beat butter, sugar, lemon, orange and vanilla extracts in large bowl at medium speed of electric mixer until creamy. Stir in flour and salt until well blended. (Dough will be crumbly.) Knead dough into smooth ball.

2. Preheat oven to 350°F. Lightly grease cookie sheets. Roll out dough, small portion at a time, to ¼-inch thickness on floured surface with lightly floured rolling pin. Cut out dough with 3-inch umbrella-shaped cookie cutter. Transfer to prepared cookie sheets.

3. Bake 12 to 14 minutes or until edges are lightly browned. Let cookies stand on cookie sheets 1 to 2 minutes; transfer to wire racks to cool completely. Decorate cookies with pink and blue icings and sprinkles for baby shower, or colors to match wedding for bridal shower. Let stand until icing is set.

makes 2 dozen cookies

yummy rattles

1½ **cups unsalted butter, softened**

1 **cup packed light brown sugar**

2 **egg yolks**

3½ **cups all-purpose flour**

1½ **teaspoons baking powder**

¼ **teaspoon salt**

Assorted colored icings, small candies and decors

1 Combine butter, brown sugar and egg yolks in medium bowl. Add flour, baking powder and salt; mix well. Form dough into ball; wrap in plastic wrap and flatten. Chill 2 hours or until firm.

2 Preheat oven to 350°F. Grease cookie sheets. Roll out dough, small portion at a time, to ¼-inch thickness on floured surface. (Keep remaining dough wrapped in refrigerator.) Cut out 24 large circles with 2½-inch round cookie cutter. Cut out 24 small circles with 1-inch round cookie cutter. Shape remaining dough into 24 (2½-inch) logs.

3 To make rattles, place large circles on prepared cookie sheets. Press 1 log at side of each circle; press small circle at opposite end of each log. Flatten logs slightly.

4 Bake 8 to 10 minutes or until edges are lightly browned. Let cookies stand on cookie sheets 1 to 2 minutes; transfer to wire racks to cool.

5 Decorate cookies with assorted colored icings, small candies and decors as shown in photo or as desired.

makes 2 dozen cookies

yummy rattles

cookie pops

1 package (20 ounces) refrigerated sugar cookie dough

All-purpose flour (optional)

20 (4-inch) lollipop sticks

Assorted colored frostings, colored glazes and decors

1. Preheat oven to 350°F. Grease cookie sheets. Remove dough from wrapper. Cut dough in half. Wrap one dough half in plastic wrap; refrigerate.

2. Roll remaining dough to ⅛-inch thickness. Cut out cookies using 3½-inch cookie cutters. Place lollipop sticks on cookies so that tips of sticks are imbedded in cookies. Carefully turn cookies so sticks are in back; place on prepared cookie sheets. Repeat with remaining dough.

3. Bake 7 to 11 minutes or until edges are lightly browned. Cool cookies on cookie sheets about 2 minutes. Remove cookies to wire racks and cool completely.

4. Decorate cookies with colored frostings, colored glazes and assorted decors as shown in photo or as desired.

makes 20 cookies

cookie pops

Kiddie creations

kids' cookie dough

1 cup butter, softened

2 teaspoons vanilla

$\frac{1}{2}$ cup powdered sugar

2$\frac{1}{4}$ cups all-purpose flour

$\frac{1}{4}$ teaspoon salt

Assorted colored glazes, frostings, sugars, sprinkles and small candies

1. Preheat oven to 350°F. Grease cookie sheets. Beat butter and vanilla in large bowl until fluffy. Add sugar and beat until blended. Combine flour and salt in small bowl. Gradually add to butter mixture until well blended.

2. Divide dough into 10 equal sections. Form shapes directly on prepared cookie sheets according to photo, or as desired, for each dough section. Bake 15 to 18 minutes or until edges are lightly browned. Cool completely on cookie sheets.

3. Decorate cookies with colored glazes, frostings, sugars, sprinkles and small candies as shown in photo or as desired.

makes 10 (4-inch) cookies

kids' cookie dough

myrtle the turtle

¾ **cup unsalted butter, softened**

¼ **cup granulated sugar**

¼ **cup packed light brown sugar**

1 **egg yolk**

1¾ **cups all-purpose flour**

¾ **teaspoon baking powder**

⅛ **teaspoon salt**

Green food color

**Assorted colored hard candies,
crushed**

**Assorted colored icings, small
candies and decors**

1 Combine butter, sugars and egg yolk in medium bowl. Add flour, baking powder and salt; mix until well blended. Tint dough green with food color; wrap in plastic wrap and refrigerate 1 hour.

2 Preheat oven to 350°F. Line cookie sheets with foil; lightly grease foil. Roll dough on floured surface to ¼-inch thickness. For turtle shells, cut dough with 4-inch round cookie cutter; cut rounds in half. Place shells 2 inches apart on prepared cookie sheets. Using hors d'oeuvre cutters, miniature cookie cutters or knife, cut out shapes in decorative pattern from shells.

3 Cut portion of remaining dough into 1-inch circles for heads. Moisten back of dough head and place at bottom center of shell; press down. Cut remaining dough into ½- to ¾-inch circles; cut circles in half for feet. Place feet on prepared cookie sheet near left and right edges of shells; press dough edges of feet and shells together gently to seal. Decorate faces with candies as desired, or leave plain to decorate after baking. Generously fill cutout shapes in shells with crushed candies.

makes 1 dozen cookies

myrtle the turtle

4 Bake 8 to 10 minutes or until edges are lightly browned and candy is melted. Transfer foil and cookies to wire racks; let cool completely. Decorate faces and shells with assorted icings, candies and decors as desired.

TIP: To crush hard candies, unwrap candies and separate into colors. Place each color in separate heavy resealable plastic food storage bag. Crush candies with rolling pin or hammer.

puzzle cookie

¾ cup shortening

½ cup packed light brown sugar

6 tablespoons dark molasses

2 egg whites

¾ teaspoon vanilla

2¼ cups all-purpose flour

2 teaspoons ground cinnamon

¾ teaspoon baking soda

¾ teaspoon salt

¾ teaspoon ground ginger

¼ teaspoon plus ⅛ teaspoon baking powder

Assorted colored frostings, colored decorator gels and assorted small candies

1 Beat shortening, brown sugar, molasses, egg whites and vanilla in large bowl until smooth. Combine flour, cinnamon, baking soda, salt, ginger and baking powder in medium bowl. Add to shortening mixture; mix well. Shape dough into flat rectangle. Wrap in plastic wrap and chill about 8 hours or until firm.

2 Preheat oven to 350°F. Grease 15½×10½-inch jelly-roll pan. Sprinkle dough with additional flour. Place dough in center of prepared pan and roll evenly to within ½ inch of edge of pan. Cut shapes into dough, using cookie cutters or free-hand, allowing at least 1 inch between each shape. Cut through dough using sharp knife, but do not remove shapes.

3 Bake 12 minutes or until edges begin to brown lightly. Remove from oven and retrace shapes with knife. Return to oven 5 to 6 minutes. Cool in pan 5 minutes. Carefully remove shapes to wire racks; cool completely.

4 Decorate shapes with frostings, gels and candies. Leave puzzle frame in pan; decorate as desired. Return shapes to openings to complete puzzle.

makes 1 large cookie

puzzle cookie

crayon cookies

1 cup butter, softened

2 teaspoons vanilla

½ cup powdered sugar

2¼ cups all-purpose flour

¼ teaspoon salt

Assorted paste food colors

1½ cups chocolate chips

1½ teaspoons shortening

1 Preheat oven to 350°F. Grease cookie sheets. Beat butter and vanilla in large bowl until fluffy. Add sugar; beat until blended. Gradually add flour and salt to butter mixture until well blended.

2 Divide dough into 10 equal sections. Reserve 1 section; cover and refrigerate remaining 9 sections. Combine reserved section and desired food color in small bowl; blend well.

3 Cut dough in half. Roll each half into 5-inch log. Pinch one end to resemble crayon tip. Place 2 inches apart on prepared cookie sheets. Repeat with remaining 9 sections of dough and desired food colors. Bake 15 to 18 minutes or until edges are lightly browned. Cool completely on cookie sheets.

4 Place chocolate chips and shortening in small resealable plastic bag; seal bag. Heat in microwave at HIGH 1 minute. Turn bag over; heat at HIGH 1 to 2 minutes or until chocolate is almost melted. Knead bag until chocolate is smooth. Cut off tiny corner of bag; pipe chocolate on cookies to look like crayons.

makes 20 cookies

crayon cookies

peanut butter and jelly sandwich cookies

1 package (18 ounces) refrigerated sugar cookie dough

1 tablespoon unsweetened cocoa powder

All-purpose flour (optional)

¾ cup creamy peanut butter

½ cup grape jam or jelly

1 Remove dough from wrapper. Reserve ¼ section of dough; cover and refrigerate remaining ¾ section of dough. Combine reserved dough and cocoa in small bowl; cover and refrigerate.

2 Shape remaining ¾ section of dough into 5½-inch log. Sprinkle with flour to minimize sticking, if necessary. Remove chocolate dough from refrigerator; roll on sheet of waxed paper to 9½×6½-inch rectangle. Place dough log in center of rectangle. Bring waxed paper edges and chocolate dough up and together over log. Press gently on top and sides of dough so entire log is wrapped in chocolate dough. Flatten log slightly to form square. Wrap in waxed paper. Freeze 10 minutes.

3 Preheat oven to 350°F. Remove waxed paper from dough. Cut dough into ¼-inch slices. Place slices 2 inches apart on ungreased cookie sheets. Reshape dough edges into square, if necessary. Press dough slightly to form indentation so dough resembles slice of bread.

makes about 1 dozen
sandwich cookies

peanut butter and jelly
sandwich cookies

4 Bake 8 to 11 minutes or until lightly browned. Remove from oven and straighten cookie edges with spatula. Cool 2 minutes on cookie sheets. Remove to wire racks; cool completely.

5 To make sandwich, spread about 1 tablespoon peanut butter on bottom of 1 cookie. Spread about ½ tablespoon jam over peanut butter; top with second cookie, pressing gently. Repeat with remaining cookies.

TIP: Cut each sandwich diagonally in half for a smaller cookie and a fun look.

under the sea

1 package (18 ounces)
   refrigerated sugar cookie
   dough

Blue liquid or paste food color

All-purpose flour (optional)

Blue Royal Icing (recipe follows)

Assorted small decors, gummy
   candies and hard candies

SUPPLIES

Pastry bag and writing tip

1 Preheat oven to 350°F. Grease 12-inch pizza pan. Remove dough from wrapper. Combine dough and blue food color, a few drops at a time, in large bowl until desired shade is achieved; blend until smooth. Sprinkle dough with flour to minimize sticking, if necessary. Press dough into bottom of prepared pan, leaving about ¾-inch space between edge of dough and pan.

2 Bake 10 to 12 minutes or until set in center. Cool completely in pan on wire rack. Run metal spatula between cookie and pan after 10 to 15 minutes to loosen.

3 Prepare Blue Royal Icing; pipe randomly over cookie to resemble wavy sea. Once icing is set, decorate with decors and candies to make sea creatures.

makes 10 to 12 servings

under the sea

BLUE ROYAL ICING

1 egg white,* at room temperature

2 to 2½ cups sifted powdered sugar

½ teaspoon almond extract

Blue liquid or paste food color

Use only grade A clean, uncracked egg.

Beat egg white in small bowl at high speed of electric mixer until foamy. Gradually add 2 cups powdered sugar and almond extract. Beat at low speed until moistened. Increase speed to high and beat until icing is stiff, adding additional powdered sugar if needed. Tint icing blue with food color, a little at a time, until desired shade is achieved.

cookie pizza

1 package (20 ounces)
    refrigerated sugar or peanut
    butter cookie dough

All-purpose flour (optional)

6 ounces (1 cup) semisweet
    chocolate chips

1 tablespoon plus 2 teaspoons
    shortening, divided

1/4 cup white chocolate chips

Gummy fruit, chocolate-covered
    peanuts, assorted roasted
    nuts, raisins, jelly beans and
    other assorted candies for
    toppings

1 Preheat oven to 350°F. Grease 12-inch pizza pan. Remove dough from wrapper. Sprinkle dough with flour to minimize sticking, if necessary. Press dough into bottom of prepared pan, leaving about 3/4 inch between edge of dough and pan.

2 Bake 14 to 23 minutes or until golden brown and set in center. Cool completely in pan on wire rack, running metal spatula between cookie and pan after 10 to 15 minutes to loosen.

3 Melt semisweet chocolate chips and 1 tablespoon shortening in microwavable bowl at HIGH 1 minute; stir. Repeat process at 10- to 20-second intervals until smooth. Melt white chocolate chips and remaining 2 teaspoons shortening in another microwavable bowl at MEDIUM-HIGH (70% power) 1 minute; stir. Repeat process at 10- to 20-second intervals until smooth.

4 Spread melted semisweet chocolate mixture over crust to within 1 inch of edge. Decorate with desired toppings. Drizzle melted white chocolate over toppings to resemble melted mozzarella cheese.

makes 10 to 12 servings

checkerboard cookie

¾ **cup butter, softened**

1 **cup sugar**

2 **eggs**

1 **teaspoon vanilla**

2¾ **cups self-rising flour**

All-purpose flour

Red and black icings

1 Beat butter and sugar in large bowl until light and fluffy. Add eggs and vanilla; stir to combine. Add self-rising flour; stir until just combined. Wrap in plastic wrap and refrigerate 30 minutes.

2 Preheat oven to 350°F. Grease cookie sheets. Roll ¼ of dough on lightly floured surface to ¼-inch thickness. Cut 24 circles with 1-inch round cookie cutter. Place on prepared cookie sheets. Bake 8 to 10 minutes or until edges are golden brown. Cool on cookie sheets 2 minutes. Remove to wire rack; cool completely.

3 Combine dough scraps with remaining dough. Roll on lightly floured surface to 12-inch square. Place on greased 15½×12-inch cookie sheet. Bake 10 to 12 minutes or until set. Cool on cookie sheet 5 minutes. Place rectangle on wire rack; cool completely.

4 Divide rectangle into 8 rows containing 8 columns. Alternate every other square with red and black icing to create checkerboard. Spread red icing on 12 round cookies and black icing on remaining 12 round cookies. Let stand until set.

makes 1 large cookie

checkerboard cookie

Acknowledgments

The publisher would like to thank the companies and organizations listed below for the use of their recipes and photographs in this publication.

Hershey Foods Corporation

Kraft Foods Holdings

Nabisco Biscuit Company

The Procter & Gamble Company

™/® M&M's, M and the M&M's Characters are trademarks of Mars, Inc. © Mars, Incorporated 2002

Unilever Bestfoods North America

Index

METRIC CONVERSION CHART

VOLUME MEASUREMENTS (dry)

$\frac{1}{8}$ teaspoon = 0.5 mL
$\frac{1}{4}$ teaspoon = 1 mL
$\frac{1}{2}$ teaspoon = 2 mL
$\frac{3}{4}$ teaspoon = 4 mL
1 teaspoon = 5 mL
1 tablespoon = 15 mL
2 tablespoons = 30 mL
$\frac{1}{4}$ cup = 60 mL
$\frac{1}{3}$ cup = 75 mL
$\frac{1}{2}$ cup = 125 mL
$\frac{2}{3}$ cup = 150 mL
$\frac{3}{4}$ cup = 175 mL
1 cup = 250 mL
2 cups = 1 pint = 500 mL
3 cups = 750 mL
4 cups = 1 quart = 1 L

VOLUME MEASUREMENTS (fluid)

1 fluid ounce (2 tablespoons) = 30 mL
4 fluid ounces ($\frac{1}{2}$ cup) = 125 mL
8 fluid ounces (1 cup) = 250 mL
12 fluid ounces ($1\frac{1}{2}$ cups) = 375 mL
16 fluid ounces (2 cups) = 500 mL

WEIGHTS (mass)

$\frac{1}{2}$ ounce = 15 g
1 ounce = 30 g
3 ounces = 90 g
4 ounces = 120 g
8 ounces = 225 g
10 ounces = 285 g
12 ounces = 360 g
16 ounces = 1 pound = 450 g

DIMENSIONS

$\frac{1}{16}$ inch = 2 mm
$\frac{1}{8}$ inch = 3 mm
$\frac{1}{4}$ inch = 6 mm
$\frac{1}{2}$ inch = 1.5 cm
$\frac{3}{4}$ inch = 2 cm
1 inch = 2.5 cm

OVEN TEMPERATURES

250°F = 120°C
275°F = 140°C
300°F = 150°C
325°F = 160°C
350°F = 180°C
375°F = 190°C
400°F = 200°C
425°F = 220°C
450°F = 230°C

BAKING PAN SIZES

Utensil	Size in Inches/Quarts	Metric Volume	Size in Centimeters
Baking or Cake Pan (square or rectangular)	8 × 8 × 2	2 L	20 × 20 × 5
	9 × 9 × 2	2.5 L	23 × 23 × 5
	12 × 8 × 2	3 L	30 × 20 × 5
	13 × 9 × 2	3.5 L	33 × 23 × 5
Loaf Pan	8 × 4 × 3	1.5 L	20 × 10 × 7
	9 × 5 × 3	2 L	23 × 13 × 7
Round Layer Cake Pan	8 × 1½	1.2 L	20 × 4
	9 × 1½	1.5 L	23 × 4
Pie Plate	8 × 1¼	750 mL	20 × 3
	9 × 1¼	1 L	23 × 3
Baking Dish or Casserole	1 quart	1 L	—
	1½ quart	1.5 L	—
	2 quart	2 L	—